Christmas in the Northern Lands

by Chuck Haavik & Aaron Kloss

DULUTH, MINNESOTA · MINNEAPOLIS, MINNESOTA

ISBN 13: 978-1-945769-00-9

Library of Congress Catalog Number: 2016911887
Printed in the United States of America
First Printing: 2016

20   19   18   17   16   5   4   3   2   1

Cover and interior design by Aaron Kloss

Published by W. I. Creative Publishing, an imprint of Wise Ink Creative Publishing.

W. I. Creative Publishing
837 Glenwood Avenue
Minneapolis, MN 55405
wiseinkpub.com

To order, visit SeattleBookCompany.com or call (734)426-6248. Reseller discounts available.

For our wives, Sally and Kathy,
who believed in us

Seated at the place of honor
In the court of the waning year
Here in northern lands,
Christmas is our most beloved feast

A precious light in
The heart of the long winter night
For it we wait and hope through
Days grown old

Like glowing embers dying low
And ancient longing arctic nights
That do not end,
Still burning in the darkness.

Through dark December solstice nights
We learn to love and seek the light,
Where Christmas light abounds
And all around is found

In homes on balsam trees that bring
Deep forest green to where we live,
On housetops and out in the
Snow-covered streets

On farms and in forests
Where nobody sees
But the fox and the raven
And chickadee

Watching alone under cool white stars
And a soft winter moon,
That fill the trees on drifting hills
With lovely pale December light

The silent gift of winter night
That calls us all to come away,
To rest awhile
And wait.

And softly and softly
An inner voice calls me
From fireplace and family
To pause for a moment
On Christmas Eve
And step outside

Where gazing up in bracing cold
All flooding with wonder
In ice candle light,
I witness the world's
Most majestic sight.

The northern night sky at Christmastime!

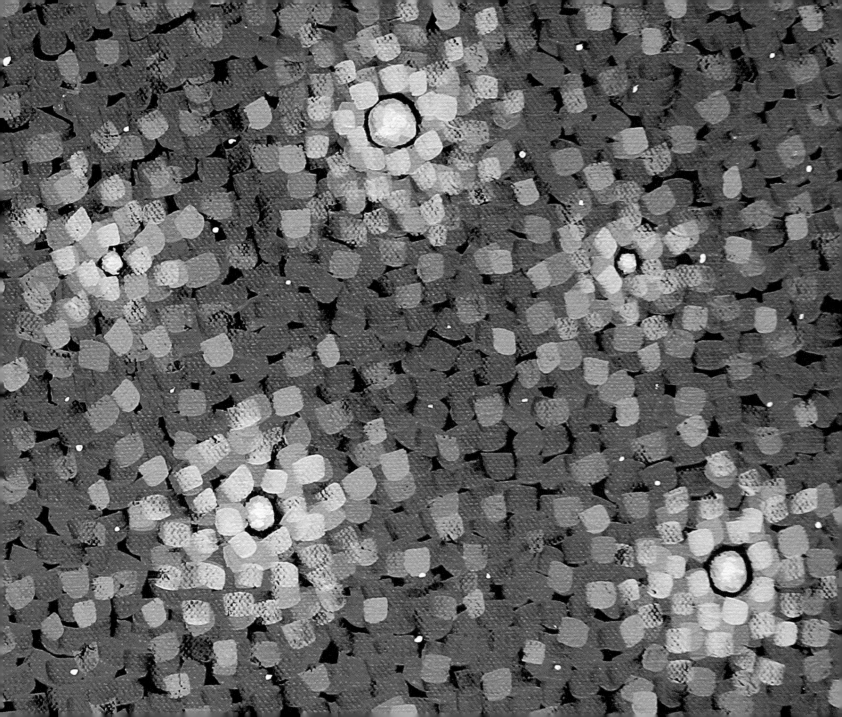

The ancient light from distant stars
That left before our world began
To meet me here this very night

In still cosmic rendezvous
All the while shining through
Breathless mosaics of
Deep purple darkness and cool winter light,
All spilling down upon
Snowy white blankets on
Billowing landscapes all
Burning alive with white crystal fire.

Such a wondrous sight,
To come at night, the mystic lights
All crashing down around
My unbelieving heart.

T hen once again at Christmastime
We bow our heads and open our hearts
And lift our voices together and sing
Of no room at the inn,
And remember the night so long ago
When love came down.

The Christmas feast is calling us home
Every fierce maiden daughter and prodigal son,
Every outcast and sinner and poor lonely soul,
We all have a place at the table tonight.

In ages past the Magi came
From ancient darkness led by a star,
The Christmas light coming into the world.

So blazing yule logs burn tonight
Their flames leaping high in the midwinter sky

For winter depths will not be borne
Without a light in the darkest night
The final days of the dying year.

Nordic darkness and northern light
Waiting winter and coming spring
Life and death and awakening,
These rhythms like wild lonely rivers
Run deep in our lives,
Given to us to hope and wait
For Christmas light to come again
Here where we live,
In a white arctic dream,
The boreal mystery we call our home.

Deep in the heart
Of Christmas lies
A living flame
Of perfect love.

One true light
In a muddy world
With a broken heart
That lights the hidden
Pathways of our hearts.

Ours is an Advent Kingdom,
Without Christmas we're just
Orphans in a winter land.

Chuck Haavik lives in Duluth on the North Shore of Lake Superior with his wife Sally, their two beautiful daughters and a yellow lab named Wilhelmina. He loves reading in front of the fireplace, walking in the woods, the smell of jasmine on a moonlit night, and the mystery of life in the great northern forests, most especially of course, watching for the light at Christmastime!

Aaron Kloss paints landscapes of the forests surrounding the home he shares with his wife Kathy and their children Miriam, Autumn & Caleb in Duluth. When he's not at the easel, he enjoys exploring the endless trails through forests filled with wildlife, rugged rock formations, majestic trees, and endless vistas full of inspiration. His paintings can be found in regional galleries and on the walls of people who share his love of the landscape.